Woman Dreamer

Preface by Ewert Cousins

A COLLECTION OF POEMS

Elizabeth-Anne Vanek

Wyndham Hall Press

WOMAN DREAMER

A Collection of Poems

by Elizabeth-Anne Vanek

Preface by Ewert Cousins

second printing, 1995

Library of Congress Catalog Card Number

89-040769

ISBN 1-55605-126-3

ALL RIGHTS RESERVED

Copyright © 1989 by Elizabeth-Anne Vanek

Printed in the United States of America

This book may not be reproduced, in whole or in part, in any form (except by reviewers for the public press), without written permission from the publisher, Wyndham Hall Press, Inc., Bristol, Indiana 46507.

To Ruth Mackelmann
who knows how to dream
and how to set others dreaming....

PREFACE

The recent decades have witnessed a remarkable awakening of spirituality. It began in the sixties with the coming of spiritual teachers from the East who touched the hearts of the younger generation disillusioned with the affluence and materialism of post-war America. The young followers of Hindu gurus and Zen masters discovered a depth of experience and a wisdom they had not found in their churches.

This sparked an awakening of spirituality in the churches. By the early seventies Christians and Jews were asking: Do we have a spiritual wisdom like that of the East? Techniques of meditation? Maps of the spiritual journey? They set out on a search for their roots and found their own spiritual heritage in the teachings of their classics: in *The Cloud of Unknowing, The Interior Castle* of Teresa of Avila, and *The Zohar.*

Since then interest in spirituality has become pervasive: in prayer groups, spiritual centers, meditation, workshops, seminars, publishing projects, academic courses. It is not surprising, then, to find poets who give expression to this awakening of spirituality. Elizabeth-Anne Vanek is such a poet. Her poetry contains a fusion of spiritual depth and poetic power; it springs from the spiritual center of the person, from that point where spiritual energy and poetic image are one. Through the poetic image she awakens the same depth in the reader.

It would be too generic to speak of her poetry as religious. Of course, it is religious, but more precisely it is that realm of religion that has been called "spirituality." This is the term that has been increasingly applied over the past decades to the deepest dimension of the person, where one is open to the transcendent, where one experiences ultimate reality, where one is in touch with God. It is here that one lives life in the Holy Spirit. Spirituality is concerned with the awakening of this inner core of the person, the dynamics of its development, and its journey to the ultimate goal.

There is reason to think that poetry is the best mode of expressing this depth of the spirit, for poetic language and imagery spring from a comparable depth of the human spirit. By her use of archetypal imagery and poetic drama, Vanek evokes in the reader this spiritual depth and guides him or her along the spiritual journey. She is perhaps at her best when she deals with Biblical themes. She has a gift for bringing a Scriptural passage or scene to life, for example, in "A Resinging of the Song of Songs" and "Nazareth Sequences."

Since the early Patristic period spiritual writers entered into the spiritual meaning of a passage chiefly through a symbolic interpretation which took its point of departure from the literal meaning of the text. By the high middle ages this symbolic interpretation had been schematized in the threefold spiritual meaning: the moral, allegorical, and analogical. Although Vanek's poetry is heir to this rich tradition, perhaps her greatest originality consists in revealing directly the spiritual meaning of the narrative level of the Biblical text. Her performance here is so effective that she has opened a whole realm of Biblical spirituality which has been largely untapped. Since most of the Bible has been written in narrative form, the reader realizes that Vanek has broken into new ground and has only just begun to explore with her unique poetic gift the wide range of spirituality embedded in the vast narrative level of Scripture.

Not all of her poems are on Biblical or explicitly religious themes. But even when she is capturing an exquisite human moment, the spiritual dimension comes through. Beyond the brush strokes of the poetic artist, one senses the same spiritual passion that energized her explicit religious themes.

Spirituality deals not only with present reality or Biblical texts. It has a history that is rooted in the very origins of the human race. That history lives in the archetypal symbols that are part of our heritage as human beings and flow through our psyches as resources for the present. In "The Tree of the Goddess," Vanek taps into these archetypal symbols with her customary vividness and dramatic power.

The reader who follows Vanek's guidance through scenes of everyday life, through the drama of Biblical narratives, and through the forest of primordial archetypal symbols, will be delighted aesthetically and enriched spiritually.

Ewert Cousins
Fordham University

TABLE OF CONTENTS

CREATION
· 1 ·

COSMIC WHEEL
· 2 ·

MICROCOSM
· 3 ·

AMBIGUITY
· 5 ·

TREE OF THE GODDESS
· 6 ·

A PSALM OF GREENING
· 9 ·

WALKING ON LAC LÉMAN, GENEVA
· 12 ·

IRREPRESSIBLE
· 13 ·

ESSENCE
· 16 ·

ATHLETA CHRISTI NOBILIS
· 17 ·

FRAGILE
· 18 ·

REALITY
· 19 ·

ARIADNE'S THREAD
· 20 ·

BENT DOUBLE
· 24 ·

PRAYER SPARKED BY A TOOTHPASTE TUBE
· 26 ·

NAILED
· 27 ·

BETWEEN YEARS
· 29 ·

PERPETUUM MOBILE
· 30 ·

THE WOUNDING
· 32 ·

SOLITARY
· 33 ·

BELOVED
· 34 ·

MESTROVIC'S PRODIGAL
· 35 ·

UNHIRED HAND
· 36 ·

INSIGHT
· 37 ·

WOMAN DREAMER
· 39 ·

A RE-SINGING OF THE SONG OF SONGS
· 57 ·

NAZARETH SEQUENCES
· 68 ·

ABOUT THE AUTHOR
· 77 ·

CREATION

In that time
in that sacred time
before memory
before story
before God cradled the earth
the Word was with God
speaking yet spoken
moving yet still
splitting light
from darkness
coaxing life
from void
dancing over the deep
rippling waters
with laughter.

And God said
"Let there be"
and there was
and there is
and there will be.
God's Word is deed.

In our time
in our sacred time
we remember God's Word
spoken tenderly--
born of flesh
born of spirit
bearing God
blazing light.
And creation trembles
at the mystery
at the power
at the glory
for grace and truth
are ours,
Alleluia!

COSMIC WHEEL

I see a wheel
luminous shafts converging
at the still hub
of the turning circle
where unitive fire
fuses differences
into explosive energy
burning
without consuming
blazing
without blinding
illuminating the darkness
in a chain-reaction
of glowing intensity.

I desire
that voracious fire
that conflagration of love;
I hunger for those sparks
of fervent flame
which burnish
add lustre
give sheen
to what is commonplace
and dull.

As the wheel spins
and the spokes turn
the fire spreads
from hub to perimeter
kindling a multitude
of paths
with its searing truth
and passionate light.

And each way
is good....

MICROCOSM

I hold
and am held by
pieces of life
ancient as humanity,
fragments of memory
which unfold wonders
teaching totemic ways,
revealing my place
in the heart of things.
I have learned
syllables of power
wielded by shamans
during hidden rites,
words sacred as spilled blood,
precious as seeds
in furrowed fields.
I know how to placate
the gods,
when to turn their wrath
and deflect their gaze
before fury erupts
in floods and fire.

I hold
and am held by
mystery
older than the race
yet always new,
always deepening,
drawing me
into that sanctuary
wider than the skies
more expansive than consciousness
yet somehow contained
within the reality
I call myself.

I hold all
and am held by all
in the cosmic embrace
which only lovers know.

AMBIGUITY

I have heard
there are ways
of knowing
what is of God
and what is not,
of distinguishing revelation
from wild imaginings
and neurological impulses.

I, for one,
recall the burning certitude
of Presence,
the searing light
of blessed assurance
and amazing grace.
I have unfastened sandals
and stood on holy ground,
cradled in fire,
absorbed in rapture.
I have known
the cloud of unknowing,
the embrace of the Bridegroom.

And yet, I am still
plagued by uncertainties
and unresolved enigmas,
pursued by darkness,
hounded down
by chaos.
The hunt is on;
frenzied dogs pant
at my heels,
leaping after me,
pitiless jaws
gaping wide as death,
and whether they are heaven-sent
or hell-bent, I will flee,
holding them at bay.

TREE OF THE GODDESS

Within the sacred grove,
flanked by myrtle and oak,
encircled by silver streams,
the Tree of Revelation stood,
boughs laden with apple clusters
dark, succulent,
heavy with mystery.

Moon-silhouetted,
it beckoned with spring fragrance
to the guardians
of the holy fire;
to the maidens
crowned with mistletoe;
to those who served cakes
piping hot
on plates of leaves,
spilling wine,
feasting on kid;
to those who danced
among flickering votive lights,
robes shining gossamer
in the star-strung night.

And the guardians
and the maidens,
servers and feasters,
dancers and revelers
beckoned in turn
to the woman
outside the circle
who gazed at the rites
of the Great Goddess.

WOMAN DREAMER

"Praise her," they said,
"for the woodlands,
for wild beasts and tame,
for the fruits of the earth.
Praise her
for the womb
from whence you have come
and to where you will return.
Praise her for wisdom
and knowledge.
Praise."

Storm clouds gathered;
the ground shook
and the woman was afraid.
Behind her, a voice rumbled:
"To eat is death,
to touch is death."
And the words had the sound
of dust about them.

But the subtle serpent,
keeper of the oracle,
caressed the tree
with its massive coils
and spoke:
"O Woman,
fear not
what is sweet to the taste
and pleasing to the eye.
This is the fruit of freedom,
gift of the Goddess
to those who choose life
in full consciousness,
to those who would destroy
both illusion and servitude.

Eat and find blessing."

Wide-eyed with wonder,
the woman,
taking the fruit,
saw mirrored in its sheen
the finger of accusation,
millennia long....
And the bite
was bitter.

A PSALM OF GREENING

From the cosmic whirl
came light
from the dance of atoms
came light
from the swelling waters
came light
and darkness was overcome.
Greening things
filled the earth,
creeping, climbing, spreading
over and upwards,
spilling blossoms
of white and hectic red,
sun yellow and royal purple,
over hills, valleys,
forests and plains.
Creatures crawled, swam,
slithered, leaped and flew,
bridling winds and waters,
taming rocks and sand,
homemakers in hollowed wood
and burrowed ground,
in rocky crevices
and the lofty limbs of pines.
And the earth teemed,
greening under the blessing
of the sun,
resounding with the songs
of countless choristers,
welcoming humankind
into a garden of delight,
wide as the universe.

II

Eons later,
here we stand
in this same garden --
time-shattered, now,

its freshness sullied,
its soil bloodied,
its resources squandered.
We stare at the strip mines
and land fills,
at dust clouds
and heaps of hazardous waste;
we hear the drone of bombers
dropping megatons of death
and smell decay
seething from the ground,
foaming in our wells,
blistering tender flesh.

III

O God, we are the stewards
of your creation,
caretakers of that greening power
running through the core
of all living things,
chroniclers of beauty, mystery,
and the ravaging of the earth.
We know the fragility
of things past--
silence of extinct species,
stillness of dead waters,
flatness of felled forests,
haunting laments
of decimated peoples.
We fear
the push-button ease
that can bring white
of eternal winter.

Give us a new greening, Lord.
Give us virescence
of aquamarine and emerald,
vegetable and olive,
berry and leaf.

WOMAN DREAMER

Let green come
from the whirl
and the dance
and the swell
of your power
that chaos may be scourged,
all shadows dispelled.

WALKING ON LAC LEMAN, GENEVA

Then, I didn't know
that flesh
is heavier than air,
more solid than water.
I thought it was a matter
of will,
of placing one foot
before the other
and watching my reflection
in the lake below.
My sister, balancing on secret ledge
under the pier,
said, "I dare you!"
and I, brave six year old,
dared and sank.

Bobbing up and down,
I heard screams
rise above laughter,
splashed, swallowed,
then surrendered
to the current,
wondering about sharks, crabs
and the distant jet d'eau.

My musings were shattered
by the abruptness
of a lame man's cane.
His words of urgency
sounded through the water
like a message
from another world
and, awakened from drifting,
I clung to his staff.

IRREPRESSIBLE

"All right," said the Cat; and this time it vanished quite slowly, beginning with the end of the tail, and ending with the grin, which remained some time after the rest of it had gone.

Alice in Wonderland

They say
I had a Cheshire-Cat smile,
an ear-to-ear grin,
wide as a Jack O'Lantern's --
and as bright.
That smile
had a life of its own,
inconvenient, at times,
when it surprised me
into trouble:
while modelling clay
in kindergarten,
I laughed at the squeeze
and squelch of ooze
and found myself
banished;
and during scoldings,
again, that smile
which brought down
harsher words
and a stronger hand.
And still I smiled,
blinking back tears,
but never allowing the corners
to twist in rage or fear.

I remember that smile,
the one I wore
at playtime
when will o'the wisps
called me "fat"

and sneered at my black hair;
I strung daisy chains,
blew the time
on dandelions,
proudly hiding
behind my smile
until weary of teasing,
they left me alone.

Waiters were charmed--
brought bowls of cherries
and ripe peaches,
extra helpings of Parmesan.
In Rome, they squeezed
my cheeks;
in Paris, they kissed
my hand.
Once, in Florence,
I gave a beggar
sugar lumps
and a smile;
startled by both,
she blessed me,
toothlessly.
Proper English ladies
said how well
I carried myself.

Later,
as plumpness
grew shapely,
my mother feared
that eager men
would read enticement
in my smile,
would see
a wanton eye
in my gaze,
but I laughed
recklessly
--and smiled.

WOMAN DREAMER

Somewhere
between childhood
and coming of age,
I lost that smile.
Perhaps it froze
in my heart
or slid away,
unnoticed.
Or perhaps
I faded,
leaving only
the smile
to face the world....

ESSENCE

On cold days,
even the sewers breathe.
I have noted vapours
wisping into thick clouds,
obscuring the road ahead.
When I am not too rushed,
I marvel how rat-infested lungs
change waste
into airy nothingness,
the stuff of dreams;
driving through swirling mists,
I am wrapped in mystery,
summoned by subtle signals
from sluices below.
Sometimes, on cold days,
I observe how my own breath
dances like the fiery speech
of a dragon
protecting its lair;
then, I muffle my face,
quickly claiming what is mine
lest the hostile world
should too readily discern
the source of my own
suspiration.

ATHLETA CHRISTI NOBILIS

Saint George's sword
plunges down the fiery gullet;
his armoured heels
trample coils of scales
and the beast--
limp-winged,
blank-eyed--
is impotent.

I, too, would be a dragon-slayer,
a hunter of brutes
and loathsome fiends,
a killer of pitiless ogres.
I would ferret them out
from the dark places,
wrenching them into the light.
There, exposed for what they are,
they would cringe,
sniveling and wilting
under my fierce gaze.
And I would wield my blade
with power,
withering them
with a victory song.

FRAGILE

I am like an egg
without a shell--
soft, easily bruised,
sensitive to the touch.
The membrane
buffering me
from the outside world
wears thin,
springs back less readily
than in days when
I could hold my own,
fight back tears,
control modulations
in my voice.
I was Spartan-born,
trained by Stoics,
formed by the British-school
of stiff upper lip
and all that,
but my invincible self
has shattered
and, like the proverbial Humpty,
I am stripped
of epidermal comfort.

REALITY

"Reality," Eliot would say,
"is too much for humankind."
Now, I know what he meant:
when all things are in focus,
sharply delineated,
freed from shadows,
when one's ears are unstopped
and one's cataracts removed,
then the knife
twists in the soul
bringing deeper clarity still
like too much sun
on a ski-slope
or intense light
after anesthesia.
Dark glasses lost,
I perceive how others
avoid my burning gaze
as though afraid
of what I might reveal,
afraid, too, of the contagion
that rawness brings

when there is too much
to bear

ARIADNE'S THREAD

I

The heat whispered
between wooden shutters,
murmured through limestone walls,
sighed under brass-knockered doors,
weighing heavily
in the dark of midnight
like an unwelcome guest.
Downstairs, the pendulum swung
in the painted clock,
past intricate flora
encased in gilt;
upstairs, as the household slumbered,
the heat insinuated itself
into her presence,
wrapping its tentacles
around arms, legs,
swathing her chest
with constricting folds
while mosquitoes droned.

Netted and snared,
she stared into the dark,
glimpsing strange shadows
flit across ancient beams.
Faces leered in knots and whorls
of time-stained lumber;
curious figures marched across wood
plundered from shipwrecks
in forgotten centuries,
journeying towards unknown lands.

And the heat
intoned a litany
of deadendedness,
saying:
"There is nothing
beyond sleep

nothing
beyond swelter
nothing
beyond nightfall,
dust to dust,
ashes to ashes;
submit
to the inevitable."

II

The tears she shed
flowed incessantly;
she could neither
think nor act
but only weep for herself
and for those who dwelled
in the house of gloom.
She looked back
and saw dust --
years of monotony
spent in idleness;
she looked forward
and saw more of the same--
a continuum
of meaningless days
and sleepless nights.

"Shall I play Rapunzel
and let down my hair?"
said she,
"Or must I spin gold
to purchase joy?
Will some Beast
exchange his heart
for a winter rose,
a kiss
for a yellow ball,
or must I sleep
a hundred years
before my prince
restores me with magic?"

And she dreamed
a thousand dreams,
captivated by images
of knights saving damsels,
slaying dragons,
breaking fetters,
unravelling mysteries
of the maze.

III

A gentle breeze
played with her hair,
teased her feet,
wafted spring fragrance
through the shutters,
startling her with possibility.
Light dispelled night's shadows,
soothed her fears;
And the breeze whispered,
"The knight and the dragon,
the pain and the power
are one;
travel the labyrinth within --
learn its intricacies,
find its centre,
discover that thread
which gives access
to perimeter and core,
allowing both the journey
and the return.
Hold the twine
of your own destiny;
trust your heart
to lead the way."

She awoke
with a song on her lips,
fire in her eyes;
and she wrenched open
the age-old shutters,

drank deeply of the morning
and began her quest
for that thread
which would lead to freedom.

BENT DOUBLE

She stood there,
eyes fixed to the ground,
back contorted
like a question mark,
limbs twisted
from the effort
of making do
with inadequacy.

She stocd there,
close to the earth,
warped and kinked
beneath ragged homespun,
humped by the weight of years,
by the scorn
of upright men
who knew sin
when they saw it --
hers, her mother's
and generations of offenses
too vile to name.

She stood there
in that holy place,
unclean and poor,
barely hearing
the jibes and jeers
of the righteous
as she waited
for chance
to save her
from the blistering burden
and the heavy heart,
from the crooked trudge
over rough terrain.

WOMAN DREAMER

She stood there,
invisible,
listening for that word
which would straighten,
unbind, disentangle,
for that creative word
to lift her eyes
to the stars
and set her dreaming.

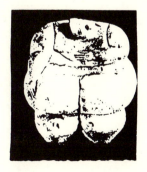

PRAYER SPARKED BY A TOOTHPASTE TUBE

You've put the squeeze on, God,
pressing, pushing down this spent tube,
tightly rolling the ends
until all excess
oozes out,
seemingly squandered.
The bent metal
writhes and twists
flecked with the paint
from a now indistinct name;
all use is gone.
What is left
testifies to ways
far above my ways,
to thoughts
higher than the heavens,
to a spilling out
so profound
that I no longer know
what fullness is
or could be.

Squeeze on, God.
Let this tube
bend
in your grip,
let it become supple
to your touch;
once again
straighten and stretch
this crushed vessel.
Let your love
be stronger
than my misshapenness;
let me thrive
under your chiropractic skill.

NAILED

Good Fridays past,
I joined the throng
of solemn worshippers
to recall the death
that made a difference,
to embrace the cross
of my crucified Lord.

Today, I would wrench
my hands
from the wood,
tearing flesh from nails
in my eagerness
to be done
with grief,
to be free
from the weight
of shadows.

Suffering Jesus,
see my hands shudder,
see them strain
for release,
jerking and pulling
this way and that,
tension knotting
pierced palms.
I would rip them loose,
cut the cords
that eat into my flesh,
leap down from this gibbet
and flee,
not turning back.

Outstretched,
bleeding freely,
open to both grace and pain,
your hands are still.

Marvelling,
I estimate
surrender's cost
and my clenched fists tremble.

BETWEEN YEARS

We like to think that
midnight splits the years,
severing old from new
with the cold efficiency
of a butcher's cleaver.
In our revelry, we proclaim
misrule's timely end--
the banishing of ill health,
lucklessness, the blues
and all that threatens
boisterous abandon.
We drink liberally,
drowning memories of setbacks,
stabs and pricks,
spilling champagne
as a libation to those gods
we hope to humour.
Sounding noise makers,
securing paper hats,
we curse enemies,
bless friends,
kiss, embrace,
bang pots and pans
while singing Auld Lang Syne.
But even as the countdown ends
and church bells peal,
I see the bloody scraps
of last year's leavings --
ghosts that will haunt,
wounds that will fester,
from one hour to the next.

PERPETUUM MOBILE

And so the wisemen
have completed their journey
yet again,
stiff from the saddle,
weary of desert storms,
bored of the incessant jangle
of camel harnesses
and of the predictable plod
of beasts of burden.
The dromedaries bend,
drop to their knees,
spitting and snorting
while travellers dismount
and disgruntled boys
unload coffers brought from afar.
The star rests
in its customary place,
illuminating the night,
beckoning with brilliance
as magi carry kingly gifts
to the peasant child
whom they have found
on Epiphanies past.
Once over the threshold,
they, too, bend,
drop to the ground,
offering themselves
in silent adoration
to the one whose name
they read in the skies.
And when, light of heart,
they return East,
they know that new signs
will summon them once more,

that new routes and caravans
will lead them
through dark days
without end.

And so the wisemen....

THE WOUNDING

Intrusive God,
you wound me most exquisitely,
piercing deep
until my heart trembles
and I grow faint,
losing all consciousness
of time, place,
color, shape,
sound or sense.

I swoon
in your embrace.
The world spins
and I know nothing
beyond the spreading wound
which is both ecstasy
and pain.

God, you have left your mark
on me,
have branded me
with your love,
burned me
with your spirit,
lanced me
with your presence.

Transfixed,
I cry out--
not for release
but for a wounding so profound
that I can lose myself
in you

and so find peace.

SOLITARY

Do you recognize
this unsmiling self
standing shadow-shrouded,
face set like flint,
eyes focussed
on nothingness?
I look for your dancing,
listen for your laughter,
but see swirling specks
of dust,
motes in sunbeams.
It is cold,
here by the frosted glass.
I stare at a winter-white world
and search for footprints,
but there are only rabbit tracks
and meaningless scratches
left by birds.
Folding my arms, I close my eyes,
imagining your embrace,
the warmth of your breath,
but my fingers find
bone beneath skin,
a new angularity,
little of softness.
There will be another day,
another time,
when you will invade my senses
with your presence,
when you will steal my heart,
thief-like,
before I know
you are near,
but today--
today I stand alone,
uncomforted,

and the tears fall . . . .

BELOVED

Don't you know
that I long for you
as you long for me,
that, I, too, yearn
for that eternal embrace
when I will hold you
so tightly
that nothing will separate
you from me
or me from you?
Gently, I will kiss your tears,
my fingers tracing away
grief's furrows
until you look up in wonder
and gaze into my eyes,
recognizing me
as the one for whom you wept
though you did not know it.
And together we shall laugh
like youthful lovers
ready to risk all
for the marriage feast;
and together we shall dance --
awkwardly at first
but in step
with the beat of our hearts
as we become accustomed
to new ways of being

together

MESTROVIC'S PRODIGAL

The prodigal returns,
cast in bronze,
utterly naked
as he kneels
before that Love
which wrenches him
from the dust.

He is weak,
this supplicant,
slight of frame,
stripped of pride
by fall
after repeated fall
into wantonness
and self-loathing.

Now, his arms reach up,
his head tilts back,
clasped by the one
to whom he clings,
the strong one
whose massive form
enfolds him
in sculpted security
and compassion.

UNHIRED HAND

I am looking for a corner
of the vineyard,
for a small patch
of untilled land,
stoney, barren,
in need of care.
I am looking
for an unassuming plot
where the laborers are few
and the grapes grow wild,
shrivelled and bitter.
My skirts are hitched,
my sleeves rolled up
and I carry fork, hoe,
shears for pruning
and a great willingness
to brave both fierce heat
and heavy rains
for the harvest's sake.

I am looking,
still looking,
weary-hearted,
sunburned and sore,
feet blistered from the trudge
between one field and the next,
but the message
is always:
"No Hired Hands Wanted"

and I keep on looking....

INSIGHT

The truth about me
is that I'm a poet --
a crafter of words
lured by magic
and mystery,
by paradox
and uncertainty.
My slice of life
is intensely buttered
on both sides,
layered with epiphanies
great and small,
spread with ambiguity,
riddled with enigmas
and breaks in consciousness.

When words come,
I am possessed by words:
they spew forth
like burning prophecy,
relentless in urgency,
generous in clarity.
They sear my lips
like Isaiah's coal,
choke me
like the scroll
on which Ezekiel fed,
until, emptied and poured out,
I find silence.

It is not so much the words
that matter
as their hidden source
deep within
the core of self,
deeper than abstract conventions
or poetic license,

deeper, too, than dexterity,
more seductive
than art or logic,
power or prestige.

I speak of the smithy
of a poet's soul,
that place where words
are forged from grace,
hammered by truth,
nailed by pain,
that place where the interplay
of light and darkness
creates both gift and curse,
laughter and anguish.

The truth about me
is that I know
how to weep
and how to dream
how to wonder
and be surprised
into joy.

I am both poem
and poet,
one who holds
the editorial pen
to censor the self
so words may be
and so, through them,
the Spirit may dance
into the hearts
of humankind.

WOMAN DREAMER

Prologue

I crawl in the dust--
in the dust
of pulverized dreams
and fractured hopes,
in the dust
of my own despair,
pursued by dreams,
hounded into the dust by dreams,
forced into the ash pit
by relentless images
and wild frenzy,
crushed by the weight
of ill-omen
and the need to prophesy.

Prostrate, I breathe dust,
taste dust
on my lips, my tongue,
hear whispers of mockery
through dust-clogged ears.
"See the woman dreamer!"
they say.
"See the one
who claims to speak for God,
who prattles peace
and babbles love,
sermonizing us all."

Raising my head,
I choke out my reply:
"Listen to me, you eyes that stare!
Listen to me, you hardened hearts,
you spirits of the dead!
I laugh at your dullness!
I rail at your apathy!"

Here, in the cavernous depths,
far from day,
I curl back into the womb
and feel my limbs
take shape once more,
skillfully knit together
by that Dreamer
who knows whether I twist or turn,
whether feet kick or thumb finds mouth.

The waters surge over me,
warm like the moonlit sea
on a summer's night;
the waters wash away
the taste of dust,
gently rocking me
with each rise and fall
of maternal breath

and I rejoice in Her heartbeat,
in the lilting song
which beckons me
to the realm of dreams;
and I leap in the womb
like the infant Baptist,
proclaiming God's glory
with my being....

Neolithic Dreamer

I, the temple priestess,
recline on the oracular bed,
eyes closed, face immobile,
full figure succulent
as a fruit for the picking,
waiting for whispers
of divine madness,
for the sacred breath
which will set eyelids flickering,

body trembling
with receptivity.
And I feel the Word
in my flesh,
hear it pulse in my blood,
know it in my heart,
until the syllables
force themselves to speech,
loosening my tongue,
unlocking my jaw,
assaulting the very air
with their power.

"God burns for you,
thirsts for you,
desires you,
longs
to place flesh, sinews
on brittle bones
that you may live.
Look into your hearts
and see the cankerous worm
rooted in rot,
the blackened places
calloused by hate,
the tightening bands
of steel
which squeeze and shrink
what breath remains.
Look
and see death!"

Then, I smell fear,
sourness of sweat,
rankness of unwashed beast;
the footsteps retreat
and I am left alone
as I always am
when the message
is more than they bargain for,
when the revelation

demands thought, action,
new ways of being,
when the dream
may swallow both dreamer
and those dreamed about...

I arise, slowly at first,
as though from drunken stupor,
and I see, before me,
spirals etched
into the place of sacrifice,
red ochre smeared
on megalithic walls.
And I remember
fragments of fantasy,
chimerical notions
that speak truth
deeper than fact.

My feet touch ground,
guiding me from shadows
into sunlight,
into the salt spray
carried by the wind.
Here, on the cliff's edge,
I untie my hair
and rest my eyes
upon the sea.

Canaanite

I dream of golden sheaves
bowing to one taller
than the rest,
thicker and more noble,
gleaming under the hot sun
like the promise of plenty
in time of famine.

WOMAN DREAMER

I dream of the stars
reverencing me,
the resplendent one,
but when I tell my dream,
my brothers, sisters,
scream, "SHAME!"
hurl curses upon my head,
because I,
younger than they,
claim glory.

"Kill the woman dreamer!
Stop up her mouth!
Break her tongue
before she silences us
with her folly!"

They tear my long-sleeved coat,
smear it with blood,
throw me into the pit
where darkness sucks me down
into deeper darkness still,
where the weight of pain
hastens my fall
until I can descend no more.

Shackled by fear,
I cry out,
hearing only
the echo of my voice
laugh like a thousand demons.
Then I bow my head.

Words come haltingly
like the speech of one
just learning how to talk.

"See my misery, God.
See how I waste away,
feasting on ashes, drinking gall.

Elizabeth-Anne Vanek

I have torn my feet on briars,
have broken my nails
while scaling stones
which hem me in.

Do not shut out my prayer
or abandon me to the dust."

In the darkness,
tears scald flesh,
sear eyes,
water my soul;
Tenderness whispers,
"My grace is enough."

All at once,
I hear the jangle of harnesses,
the plod of camel trains,
Ishmaelites from Gilead
bearing balsam and resin
to the land of Egypt.

Dreamer in Egypt

I dream of my father's flock
pasturing at Shechem,
of the choice grapes
of the Hebron Valley,
of Dothan, place of two wells
where I was plucked
from my former life
in my seventeenth year.
I can no longer sing
songs of festival
or sound praise
upon my harp
for my heart

cracks with grief,
remembering Canaan.

I am the alien,
the woman dreamer,
who looks upon the Nile,
upon the rich black silt,
yearning for desert days
of simple shepherding.
Here, I wear Pharaoh's ring,
interpret dreams,
govern the land,
but my thoughts
are with my people
whose crops wilt,
withering to dust-dry roots
in sun-cracked earth.

When they come,
will my sisters know me?
Will my brothers
remember their sin
or give me a coat
to equal my father's gift?
Can they restore
my lost years
or make me forget
the taste of power?
They will bow before me
and I will give them bread,
hiding my tears.

Fish Song

In the belly of Sheol
I cannot dream
lurched as I am
this way and that
through surging waters.

God touched my mouth
but I would not speak,
would not warn Nineveh
of the wrath to come.
And the divine will
became a violent squall,
whipping up the sea,
splintering oars, masts,
until, filled with dread,
the sailors cast me
into the turmoil
where God's great fish
swallowed me whole.

Dreams do not come
when one resists
the message or
persists in stubbornness.
Fear entangled me,
binding my feet,
numbing my heart
until I no longer heard
the word within.

"I will not prophesy!"
I said,
"I will not play the fool."

I had dreams of my own--
days of ease,
ordinary days
of well-side gossip
and women's ways,
days for flaunting braceleted arms
before admiring eyes,
for displaying finely-woven cloth,
the labor of my hands
to those less skilled.
I would grind corn,
bake bread fit for Elijah,

would braid the young girls' hair,
sing to the little ones.

Humble dreams--
no flights of fancy
or wild frivolity,
but simply the hope
that I could do
what women have always done
when left in peace.

But I was torn
from my native soil,
sent to the wicked city
to preach repentance,
not because
of special gifts,
but simply at God's whim.

It was not the painted harlots
who made me run,
nor thieving hawkers
with weighted scales,
nor even cunning beggars
with sham infirmities.
Rather, I fled the iron will
and hardened heart,
atrophied minds
and soulless eyes,
those who trampled life
beneath indifferent feet,
warmongers all....

"Let me be!" I prayed,
but God tracked me down,
relentless as a lover
forsaken by his beloved....

Now, on the third day
of my entombment,

I know who has won
this wrestling of wills.
"I am yours," I say.
"My word shall be your word.
My dream shall be your dream.
I will speak in your name."

Blood flows in my veins
once more;
my limbs, no longer stiff,
stretch and flex
in this cramped space
until fish ribs crack and strain
and the tortured beast
retches in misery,
hurtling me
upon the Tigris' shores.

Captive in Babylon

In the palace of Babylon,
I balk at the royal table,
preferring dust to defilement,
lowering my eyes
under insolent stares,
conscious of female form,
desirous of no man.

They changed my name,
instructed me in Chaldean lore,
but could not turn my heart
from my beloved,
away from the living God.
Each day of fast
brings wisdom, grace,
the presence of my Lord.
Sages, diviners, soothsayers
are spellbound by my words
when I reveal dreams,

decipher visions,
unravel mysteries
beyond the ken of court magicians.

They ask me
to account for what I am,
to name angelic mentors
or secret witchery,
to share hidden craft
or magic scripts
as though the words I speak
can be explained, dissected,
subjected to reason.

"Kill the woman!" they say.
"Set a trap for her
lest we be shamed."

I have eaten my fill
of wailings, moanings
and lamentations,
have devoured the scroll
word by word
until it cloys
in my throat
and I gag,
spewing out bitterness
through lips burned
by the seraph's coal.

But as I speak,
they stop up their ears,
shun me like a leprous thing,
avoid my searing gaze.

"A woman of passion!" they say.
"Frenetic, eccentric--
lock her away!"

Whether they heed or not,
I am compelled to speak,
burdened as I am
by that heavy Word
which wearies me,
by that Word
which eats at my heart
until I can restrain it
no more.

I name their sin,
not claiming innocence
but simply speaking
what comes
in waking and dreaming.
They spit at me,
tear at their hair,
gather jagged stones
to hurl in the night.

Veil shimmering,
I have danced
in the heart of flames,
unscathed,
fanned by God's spirit,
cooled by wind and dew
while servants hot with fury
stoked the furnace,
heaping oil, pitch, brushwood
until they themselves
were destroyed.

I have seen dynasties fall,
the king grow mad,
have observed the toppling of princes,
the defeat of the dragon,
have survived jaws
of famished lions
in a pit of whitened bones.

WOMAN DREAMER

They would tear me
limb from limb
not because I prophesy
but because I am woman --
bold, self-assured,
pregnant with God's word.

How can a woman," they say,
"Speak for the Lord of Hosts?
How can a woman
speak for the God of armies?"

And I laugh
at their folly,
mocking the idol
they have made of war,
spitting on their swords
of burnished bronze.
And I pray to the Creator,
the compassionate one,
whose love
is the child I bear.

Now, the writing on the wall
spells out disaster;
the fingers move,
wedging cuneiform
in relentless stone
like bird tracks upon sand,
and I turn to the trembling king.

"O mighty one," I say,
"I, the woman dreamer,
want neither gold
nor purple robes,
neither rings nor amulets.
The words I speak
are freely given;
the price
is what you yourself
will pay for bloated pride.

Elizabeth-Anne Vanek

Here, in this banquet hall,
you have polluted Jerusalem,
stained sacred vessels
with indifference,
applauded false gods,
laughed at the lewd songs
of your minstrels.

The most high God
has found you wanting;
you have been weighed...."

Dream Feast

My friends,
gather for the dream.
Trumpets sound silver,
the shofar calls.
The feast of fat foods
and fine wines is spread;
the meal awaits.
Your place is set,
and the Bridegroom comes.

Do you not hear his feet
gentle upon the mountain?
Flowers yield fragrance;
earth trembles;
trees bend as he draws near
strewing blossoms before him
to carpet the way.
Stones soften beneath his step;
streams run, leap,
cascading down rock
while rainbows arc
in the spray.

Come! Come speedily!
Leave your tent-making,

your spinning and fishing,
your selling and haggling.
Leave fields and pastures,
temples and synagogues.
Leave the sheep in their pen,
chickens to their scratching,
turtledoves in the temple court.
Leave villas and hovels,
city streets and dusty tracks.
Leave all and come!
The Bridegroom draws near.

Come! Come as you are!
Bring nothing but yourselves.
Leave behind canes and crutches,
money bags, jewels,
phylacteries and beggars' cups.
Come! Come empty.

Unclench your fists!
Stretch out your hands
to claim the inheritance --
here there is room for you
and for all who have known
the swollen belly and parched tongue,
the aching heart and weary feet,
the closed door and unsmiling face.
Here is a feast for the poor.

Come! Come speedily!
Do you see how the grapevines
have labored?
Each branch bears one thousand twigs,
each twig one thousand grapes,
each grape yields a barrel of wine.
See how rich! Taste how purple!
The vineyard's lord
tends fields with care,
keeping guard at the watch tower,
driving away thieves, wild beasts,
those who would steal the harvest.

For his sake,
I have worked the grape press
day after day
through months and years
of aching limbs and blistered flesh.
Now wine flows like water.

Take, drink to his coming,
the cup offered by woman's hands
for you
and for the world,
wine poured out
in memory of the Christ,
in discovery of who we are.
Drink
that daughters, sons,
may learn.

Do you see how the wheat
bends to the earth
laden with plenty?
Each stalk bears one thousand ears,
each ear yields one thousand loaves,
each loaf feeds one thousand people.
When the Bridegroom comes,
we will know fullness,
the taste
of his presence.

Take, eat,
bread made by woman's hands,
bread offered by woman's hands
for you
and for the world.
How I have dreamed
of breaking this bread with you
-- the stuff of our lives,
fragmented yet whole.
Eat. There is unity
in the crumbs.

WOMAN DREAMER

How I have longed
for this feast,
for this gathering
of exiles.
Here are white robes!
Here, olive wreaths
and vigil lamps!
Trample your weapons
and put on peace,
for I hear
the bridesmaids rejoicing,
I feel the ground shake,
weighted down
by majesty.

Do you hear the caverns roar?
Now he drags Death
from the realm of dark dreams
and will serve him as steaks,
chaos dismembered,
slaughtered and cooked
that we may remember
and live,
weeping no more.

Now he straightens the bent
and mends the broken.
Now he embraces outcasts
and frees the oppressed.
The hosannas ring
and he draws near.

Do you not see him
gentle upon the mountain,
fanned by the four winds.
robed in the sun?
Are not your hearts
pierced by his gaze,
wounded by his love?
Does not your flesh
tremble at his coming?

Gather for the dream,
for the lavish feast --
the Beloved is here.
Alleluia.

A RE-SINGING OF THE SONG OF SONGS

In the half-light,
white-robed,
eyes wide with dreaming,
I saw his shadow
through the slats
of wooden shutters
and my heart beat wildly,
recognizing
the one I loved.
And the shadow
illumined
the darkness,
casting its light
upon my hiding place;
finding myself discovered,
I lowered my gaze --
and he was gone.

On my bed,
through that long night,
I thought of him.
The mosquitoes droned
incessantly
and at dawn,
when I listened
for his voice,
I heard instead
the rattle of country carts
heading for market,
the crack of the whip,
the jangle of lanterns
and harnesses,
the tired curses
of early risers.

I have risen too late,
waited too long
beneath tear-drenched sheets,
wrapped in pride,

numbed by grief.
Once he stood
behind this wall,
peered through this window,
but I shrank
into the dark recesses
of my room,
frightened
by what he might ask
and how I would respond.

"Do not awaken my love,"
I whispered to the shadow,
"Do not stir me
before my time."

But he set his eyes
upon me
and I burn
at the memory
of tenderness
and quiet love
too sweet
to bear.

In the half-light,
as he stretched his hands
towards me,
it seemed he wept
while I, overcome,
turned my head
to the wall.

My beloved has gone
and I am sick
with love.
Crimson has faded
from my cheeks, my lips;
the fragrance
from my hair.
My soul fails
at his flight --

WOMAN DREAMER

I seek him
but do not find him,
I call him
but he does not answer.

And so I veil myself
in mourning,
buckling my sandals
against the stony ground
which summons me,
tightening my belt
against lean and hungry days
in unknown lands.

Tearfully, I take my leave
of the song bird,
stroking its yellow breast
before letting it soar
from the wicker cage.
I pick dead heads
from pink geraniums
one last time,
sprinkle pots of rosemary
for remembrance,
then kiss my sisters
where they lie sleeping,
gently, lest they awake
and hold me back.

In the rose-scented morning,
I drink deeply
from the fountain,
pluck ripe figs
to break my fast,
a sprig of orange blossom
for my hair
and, carrying nothing,
follow the path
through the garden gate,
out to the dusty street.

Elizabeth-Anne Vanek

"Have you seen him
whom my heart desires?"
I ask the peasant women
in brightly woven
skirts and shawls;
they stare at me,
then shake their heads,
scurrying on with baskets
of eggs and cheese,
anxious for profit.

I follow them
like some dark wraith,
observing the sway of their hips,
the deep cracks
in their bare feet,
as we, market-bound,
leave behind
vineyards, olive groves
and ancient farms.

"Have you seen my Beloved?"
I ask in the village square
but my voice is lost
in the haggling
for dull-eyed rabbits
and strings of garlic,
for potent amulets
and lengths of cloth.
Over the hawkers' cries,
the church bells sound
and for a moment
I think I hear a whisper
carried by the wind:
"Come, then, my love,
my lovely one, come."

I strain my ears
but it is gone,
and I am mocked
by a donkey's bray,
by the toothless smiles

of old tobacco chewers.
The pigeons swoop
for grain
and I drift on,
listlessly....

The sun is merciless
but there is no shade
along the shore.
The sand burns
between my toes
and my head reels
with midday madness.
Again, I hear the whisper,
"Come, then, my love,
my lovely one, come,"
and I stumble
towards the water,
filled with desire.

Casting off my clothes,
I plunge
into the waves,
diving deep
into the bluest depths
until I think
my lungs will burst,
deeper, deeper,
past schools of Red Flames,
past rocks clad with sea urchins,
pale anemones and trailing weeds,
right to the silver ridges
where lie the starfish,
clams and creeping hermits.

Breaking the surface
once more,
I gasp for air,
heart pounding,
eyes burning,
the taste of salt
upon my lips,

a ringing in my ears.
My arms are empty,
my hands clutch at nothingness
and still I hear
the refrain,
"How beautiful you are,
my love, how beautiful...."

Clawing at sand,
I drag myself
from the sea,
sinking upon shell fragments
scattered where beach
meets waves.
The water laps over me,
swirling strands
of long black hair
in surging foam;
I close my eyes,
surrendering to the gentle
ebb and flow
of dreams....

Rested, I set sail
this summer's night
when the cliffs loom orange
under the August moon,
when the sea gleams
like a sheet of gold foil,
utterly still.
And I leave behind
the yellow song bird,
the pink geraniums,
my fine clothes
and noble name.
I say no goodbyes,
shed no tears
but turn my face
to the west,
towards the new land
from where my beloved beckons.

His voice ripples across the waters:
"Come, come,
my lovely one,
my only one...."

and I whisper love songs
to the wind.

II

The wind is bitter here,
icy like the tentacles
which grip my heart,
squeezing out hope.
I followed his song
across land and ocean
until at last,
weary, tempest-tossed,
I sailed past Liberty
to join the throngs
of homeless ones
waiting for process.

Now, an alien,
I walk winding city streets,
faceless, nameless,
lost in the shadows
of tall towers
which grasp for the sky
proudly, like Babel.
I am numbed by traffic din,
by the pressing crowd
which elbows and jostles
but knows no intimacy
as it rushes
without mind or soul,
a beast on the rampage.

Lights flash out enticements,
luring passers-by

into sanctuaries
of opulence.
I am mesmerized
by speed and glitter,
by the easy exchange
of goods and gold,
by the revolving doors
of gourmet palaces,
by blind men playing trumpets
on busy corners.

I forge ahead,
wrapped in smog,
choked by tears,
greeted by vacant eyes
or by the insolent stares
of foolish old men
who still crave tender flesh,
the feel of a woman.
I have neither words
nor smiles
to waste on them;
I cannot bring myself
to ask
if they have seen
the one I seek.

They would say,
"What makes your beloved
better than other lovers?
Are his arms so strong,
his kiss so sweet?
Does he sing
wild gypsy songs
which stir your blood,
making frenzy so flow
in your veins
that your feet
cannot resist the dance
or your heart
his?"
And so I hold my tongue

lest the city watchmen
beat me, wound me,
strip me of my cloak....

Loneliness aches like hunger,
gnawing at my flesh, my bones,
until I am overcome
with grief
for all I have left behind.
Do my sisters
weep for me still?
Will the geraniums bloom
or the yellow bird
warble its sweet song?
Here, there are birds, flowers,
for the asking,
but they do not
cheer my heart.
I would wish
for a deep forgetting,
but the smell of rosemary
dances in the wind....

There is water here
but it is cold
like the North Sea,
lacklustre,
fit for sleek yachts
with white sails.
There is neither cobalt
nor turquoise,
no Mediterranean depths
sparkling fathoms deep
with mystery,
no red and yellow fishing boats
with painted eyes
to ward off evil
and discern the haunts
of tuna and mackerel.
There are no sun-browned fishers
bent over lobster pots
and crudely woven nets of hemp.

Elizabeth-Anne Vanek

I thirst for salt spray,
for the rough red wine
of fertile valleys;
I hunger for black-crusted loaves
smeared with tomatoes, oil,
capers and olives,
spiced hot with basil
and freshly-grated pepper.
I long for fireworks
honouring village saints,
for nougat and honey rings
sold at festas,
for candles burning
in wayside churches,
for terraced fields of prickly pear,
for carob trees
overhanging rubble walls....

I am worn with longing;
I am sick with love,
but there is no going back,
no going forward
without healing.
And so I will carry
the memory of a time
and of a place,
the sound of his voice;
I will shear my hair
and earn my bread,
here in this foreign land.
And if, by chance,
my beloved once more
looks in the window,
peers through the lattice,
I will say,
"Feed me with raisin cakes,
restore me with apples."

Seeing my tears,
he will say to me,
"Come, then, my love,
my lovely one,

for see, winter is past,
swallows return,
green things bud,
and flowers brighten the earth."

NAZARETH SEQUENCES

They do not know.
They have not seen.
They have neither felt
nor touched nor tasted
the power and glory
of owning and letting go
of being and letting be.
They have not probed
beneath the skin
for subtle signs of mystery
or studied the harmony
of opposites
present in yin and yang,
animus and anima.

They have not heard
life's rhythms
pulse beneath the rain-drenched earth
or whisper in the greening leaves
of lilacs and magnolias;
they have not smelled its fragrance
carried by the wind
caressed by gentle breezes;
nor have they felt its beat
throbbing in the heart of a child.

No. They have seen only
boundaries, barriers
and dichotomies --
rifts between body and soul,
man and woman,
saved and damned,
divisions wide as gaping canyons,
bloody as war.

They dwell in a crumbling house,
teetering on termite-ridden frame.
Their resources dwindle in trade;
they lavish wages on refuse,

remembering neither their beginning
nor their ending,
nor the days in between;
neither kairos nor chronos
nor things of significance.

What **they** know
are limits and restrictions,
brick walls without doors,
concrete cells sans windows.
For them, life is function,
rote and predictable;
their god, Big Brother,
omniscient, omnipotent,
the feared puppeteer
who pulls the strings
this way and that,
jerking obedience
from wooden manikins.

II

The voice that first whispered
surprised the child
with tenderness.
"Come," said the voice.
"Come into the wonder of yourself.
Descend deep
into the garden
of blessing
where the taste of the apple
is life
where the choice of the serpent
is life
where the toil of the earth
is life
where the swelling of the womb
is life not curse.

Come, let the laughter of God
rouse you to hilarity;
let the clay in your hands
take flight and warble --
a rainbow of birds
for the garden,
each plumed and crested
with iridescence."

And the child
ran to the garden
and heard the stars sing.
The stream rippled
in blue melody
while supple willows
bent their branches
to the dance.

"Come," said the voice.
"Find yourself in stardust
and earth,
in rose petals
and daisy chains.
Weave for yourself
a diadem of forget-me-nots.
Let the rain
bathe you
with grace."

And the child
grew in wisdom,
descending ever more deeply
into that centre
where tree, cross and axis
are one,
where self and other
merge indivisibly,
taking on essence of sky and sea,
soil and flame.
And the child laughed and danced,
playing in that garden of delight

prepared for her
before time began.

III

"Go," said the voice.
"Go back
to that place bound
by calendars,
shackled by schedules,
strangled by efficiency.
Go to that place
where they neither see nor hear,
feel nor understand,
where words mean little
and smiles come cheaply.
Go. Say to them
that the garden beckons
both at midday
and at midnight,
both at dawn and at dusk,
at the hour of now.

For now
is the time
of the garden,
the hour of holiness,
the time to redeem
from forgetfulness,
the time of waiting
in readiness.

Now is the time
for cutting loose
and disentangling,
for unfettering
and extricating,
for opening wide
the iron cage....

Tell them
to descend
deep
into the mystery
of who they are,
deep, deep
into the dark
where deeper darkness
burns, refines like fire,
yielding to deeper darkness still
until all is consumed
by the purgatorial flame
and only light remains.

In dissolution
is plentitude,
in destruction,
quickening.
They will rise
like the Phoenix,
brilliantly arrayed
in gold and purple;
fresh from immolation,
they will ascend
to the altar of the sun.

Go, go at the present hour,
at the hour of now.
Go swiftly
and speak my word."

IV

In the midst of the elders,
the child unrolls the scroll.
Tight lipped,
they watch with narrowed eyes;
arms folded, puffed up with pride,
they wait,
clothed in black,

garbed in self-righteousness,
an assembly of scorpions
with poised stings.

"This is the word I received,"
says the child.
"This is the word I heard
in waking and dreaming,
the creative word
which calls forth life,
commanding all things to be
and to be still,
to know who is God;
that word high above all words
which scatters reason
to the winds,
summoning compassion
from the swelling heart.

Have you seen eyes
brimming deep
like wounds
in the world's surface?
Have you seen them ooze
endless tears,
ravaging beauty
with salty rivulets?
The face crumples,
the tears fall
and the wounds
gape wide --
see the God
who weeps for you
and for the world.

See those eyes
brimming deep,
inviting you
into the fraility of love.
You must come naked and poor,
clad only

in anguish,
marked by the badge
of affliction.

Why spill your life
on what will consume you?
Why squander yourself
on what fails to satisfy?
Come, come into the garden
where the river
serpentines its way
through lush valleys,
watering the flood plains,
impregnating the very stones.
Come to where the day lilies
linger through eons
and what was thought ephemeral
blooms eternally.
Come to where your thirst
will be slaked,
your hunger sated."

Her words
burn their hearts
charring stoney edges
with fire;
their eyes smoulder
in sunken sockets
black with hatred
and seething rage.

"Is this child and daughter mad,
possessed by Beelzebub
and the spirit of Baal?
A thousand fiends
crawl in her soul,
spawning maggots
of perfidy,
unbinding her fool's tongue
so that it spews
iniquity upon iniquity,
blasphemies untold.

WOMAN DREAMER

A thousand lies
lurk in her smile,
cunningly designed
to disarm the righteous.
Away with her!
She undermines the nation
with her very breath.
Chaos springs from her bowels;
she is the devil's gateway,
a blot on the light of day."

Grinding teeth, tearing hair,
they seize the child,
pinching and pummelling
tender flesh,
cuffing, scoffing,
kicking, spitting,
buffeting her head, her face,
bruising her bones
until she lies bloodied
and silenced,
a heap
of broken humanity
surrounded by jagged stones.

"Come," says the voice
trembling with sorrow,
"Come. Come back to the garden
for now is the hour of healing,
the hour of grace.
Shake the dust from your feet
and live;
I will anoint your wounds,
binding your hurts.
You will sing
once more
and I will raise my voice
with yours,
in harmony.
You will find rest
in my embrace."

76   Elizabeth-Anne Vanek

   And the child smiles
   through her tears....

ABOUT THE AUTHOR

Elizabeth-Anne Vanek was born in England but spent most of her childhood on the island of Malta in the Mediterranean. Following her marriage to a Peace Corps volunteer, she moved to the U.S. in 1974 where she has enjoyed a varied career: teaching English at DePaul University, Graduate Religious Studies at Mundelein College and poetry at Express-Ways Children's Museum; writing articles on liturgy, scripture, spirituality and creativity for religious journals; giving workshops on creative writing and religious topics to faculties and church groups; serving as a poetry advisor to The International Commission on English in the Liturgy's (ICEL) subcommittee on the liturgical psalter; offering spiritual direction and retreats....

Vanek, who holds a D.Min. from the Graduate Theological Foundation, is the author of two other poetry collections: **Extraordinary Time** (1988) and **Frost and Fire** (1985), both published by Life Enrichment Publishers, Canton, Ohio. She and her husband, Jim, live in Chicago with their children, Peter and Alexia.